THE BEST HEALTHY DOG FOOD COOKBOOK

How to Safely Make Easy Nutritious Meals for Your Best Friend

TESSA MARKS

THE BEST HEALTHY
DOG FOOD COOKBOOK

As loving pet parents, we always strive to provide the best care for our dogs, and a vital aspect of that care is their diet. While many commercial dog foods on the market offer balanced nutrition, the choice to cook at home for your dog is an individual decision that can have its own set of rewards and benefits.

It's important to acknowledge that not all commercial dog foods are created equal, and some brands offer high-quality, nutritionally complete options.

However, the growing interest in homemade dog food stems from a desire to have greater control over the ingredients and quality of the food we provide our furry friends. This fresh food cookbook aims to guide you through creating delicious, wholesome, and well-balanced meals for your dog, all in the comfort of your kitchen.

By choosing to cook at home for your dog, you can ensure their diet is tailored to their needs and preferences. In addition, you'll have the opportunity to select whole-food ingredients that are fresh, minimally processed, and packed with essential nutrients.

Moreover, homemade dog food allows you to monitor and adjust the recipes based on your dog's health, age, activity level, and dietary restrictions.

In this cookbook, we'll explore a variety of recipes and tips for creating fresh, nutritious meals for your dog. From the essential vitamins and minerals to incorporating a balance of proteins, carbohydrates, and fiber, we'll cover everything you need to know to prepare homemade dog food confidently.

So, grab your apron, and let's embark on this exciting journey together, providing your dog with the love and nourishment they deserve through the joy of home cooking.

TABLE OF CONTENTS

CHAPTER 1

THE POWER OF FRESH DOG FOOD

THE IMPORTANCE OF FRESH INGREDIENTS IN YOUR DOG'S DIET

Fresh ingredients are essential for your dog's health and well-being as they provide numerous benefits compared to the processed or artificial alternatives. Some of the research-backed benefits of fresh dog food include the following:

- Maintaining a healthy weight: Fresh dog food, made from high-quality ingredients, can help manage your dog's weight, preventing obesity-related health issues.
- Improved digestive health: Unprocessed food is often easier for your dog to digest, reducing the risk of gastrointestinal problems and promoting a healthy gut microbiome.
- Better quality poop: Fresh food can result in smaller, firmer, and less odorous stools, indicating improved digestion and nutrient absorption.
- Higher quality sleep: A diet of wholesome ingredients can lead to better sleep quality for your dog, which is essential for their overall health and well-being.
- Improved cognitive function: Fresh food can provide essential nutrients that promote brain health and cognitive function, especially in aging dogs.
- Optimal muscle maintenance: A diet with 60-70 percent protein-rich animal ingredients can support muscle maintenance and overall health in dogs.
- Whole fruits and vegetables: Fresh dog food can include whole fruits and vegetables, which provide essential vitamins, minerals, and antioxidants for optimal health.

In summary, incorporating fresh ingredients into your dog's diet can significantly improve their overall health, digestion, cognitive function and quality of life. However, you must consult your veterinarian to ensure you provide a balanced and appropriate diet for your dog's specific needs, like allergies, anxiety, gastrointestinal infections, obesity, insomnia, and other health issues.

PROTEINS

Proteins are essential nutrients for dogs, playing a crucial role in maintaining their overall health and well-being. They build and repair muscles, grow and keep tissues, and perform various essential bodily activities.

Proteins are one of the six essential nutrients required for dogs, along with water, fats, carbohydrates, minerals, and vitamins. These nutrients are involved in all the vital functions of a dog's body and are required as part of their regular diet.

When feeding your dog, it is important to provide adequate protein intake to ensure their bodies function smoothly and maintain optimal health. The amount of protein each dog requires depends on age, size, activity level, and overall health.

It is important to consult with a veterinarian when feeding a fresh food homemade diet to determine the appropriate protein intake for your specific dog and ensure their dietary needs are met.

Dogs can benefit from a variety of protein sources in their diet. Some of the top protein choices for dogs include:

Chicken: Chicken is a widely available and easily digestible protein source in dog food.

Beef: Beef is another popular protein option for dogs, providing essential amino acids and a taste that appeals to a dog's palate.

Pork: Pork is a nutritious and easily digestible protein source, making it a suitable option for dogs.

Fish: Fish provides essential omega-3 fatty acids, which are beneficial for a dog's skin, coat, and overall health.

Poultry (other than chicken): Other types of poultry, such as turkey and duck, can also serve as protein sources for dogs.

Organ meats: Hearts, livers, kidneys, and lungs from various animals can be nutritious sources of protein for dogs.

Eggs: Eggs are high in protein, fatty acids, and vitamins, making them a beneficial addition to a dog's diet. However, it's important to note that approximately 4% of dogs may be allergic to eggs.

Grains and oilseeds: Some grains, like corn and wheat, and oilseeds, such as soybeans, can also provide protein for dogs. However, these plant-based proteins may not be as bioavailable or complete as animal-based-ones.

A balanced diet that meets your dog's nutritional needs and preferences is essential. If your dog has specific dietary restrictions or allergies, consult your veterinarian to determine the best protein sources for their requirements.

FRUITS

Dogs can enjoy a variety of fruits as low-calorie, nutrient-rich treat. However, always remember to feed fruits in moderation to avoid health issues. Here are some fruits your furry friend can safely savor:

Bananas: This potassium, vitamin, biotin, fiber, and copper-rich treats can be enjoyed in moderation by your dog. They're low in cholesterol and make for a delightful snack.

Blueberries: Packed with antioxidants and fiber, they are a healthy addition to your dog's diet, supporting their digestive system and overall well-being.

Cucumbers: Low in calories, cucumbers make a refreshing snack, especially for dogs needing to shed a few pounds.

Mangoes: Nutrient-dense and full of carotenoids, fiber, potassium, and vitamins A, B6, C, and E, mangoes are a tropical treat for your pup. Remember to remove the skin and pit before serving.

Pineapples: Rich in vitamins, minerals, and fiber, pineapples can be a tasty treat for your dog. Just make sure to remove the skin and core first.

Raspberries: These fiber-rich fruits help improve your dog's digestion and fight obesity by keeping them fuller for longer. The antioxidants in raspberries also support your dog's immune system and overall health.

Apples: A crunchy delight that can improve your dog's dental health and freshen their breath. Packed with fiber, vitamins C, A, and K, and minerals like zinc and iron, apples offer various benefits. Just remember to remove any seeds and cores.

Watermelon: Watermelon is not only a delicious and hydrating fruit for humans, but it's also a healthy treat for dogs. This refreshing fruit is low in calories and packed with essential nutrients such as vitamins A, B6, and C and potassium. Both red and yellow watermelons are safe for most puppies and adult dogs to enjoy. When introducing new fruits to your dog's diet, do so gradually and watch for any signs of allergies or digestive issues.

Including fruits and vegetables in your dog's meals can provide various nutritional benefits. Blueberries, for instance, are an excellent source of dietary fiber, antioxidants, and vitamin C, which help boost your dog's digestive and immune systems while supporting healthy brain function. So go ahead and add a fruity twist to your dog's mealtime!

VEGGIES

Adding some veggies can provide extra vitamins and nutrients. Vegetables can also serve as low-fat and healthy meal toppers or treat replacements for dogs on weight loss programs. Here are some popular vegetables you can include in your dog's meals.

Sweet Potatoes: Rich in vitamins and minerals, sweet potatoes are an excellent source of dietary fiber and antioxidants.

Potatoes: These starchy vegetables can provide energy and essential nutrients for your dog, but they should be served cooked and in moderation.

Carrots: Low in calories and high in fiber and vitamins, carrots make a crunchy and nutritious treat for your dog.

Green Beans: Packed with vitamins and minerals, green beans are a low-calorie and filling option for your dog's diet.

Peas: These small legumes are a good source of protein, fiber, vitamins, and minerals.

Broccoli: This nutrient-dense vegetable is rich in vitamins, minerals, and fiber but should be served in moderation due to its potential to cause digestive issues in large quantities.

Beets: High in antioxidants, beets can support your dog's overall health. Make sure to cook them before serving them to your dog.

Corn: A common ingredient in dog food, corn is a source of carbohydrates, fiber, and various nutrients. However, avoid feeding your dog corn on the cob, as the cob can be a choking hazard.

Kale: A leafy green vegetable, kale is rich in vitamins, minerals, and antioxidants. Introduce it gradually to your dog's diet to avoid digestive issues.

Spinach: Another leafy green, spinach is packed with nutrients and can be a healthy addition to your dog's diet. However, it should be served in moderation due to its high oxalate content.

When preparing vegetables for your dog, cook them without salt or seasoning and cut them into small, manageable pieces to avoid choking hazards.

FISH

Fish is an excellent source of protein and healthy fats for dogs. However, not all fish are created equal, and some types may contain high levels of mercury or other toxins. It's important to choose safe and nutritious fish for your furry friend. Here are some of the best types of fish for dogs:

Salmon: This fatty fish is an excellent source of omega-3 fatty acids, which help support healthy skin and coat, reduce inflammation, and boost the immune system. Fresh or canned salmon can be given to dogs, but avoid salmon that has been seasoned or contains bones.

Whitefish: This mild-flavored fish is rich in protein and low in fat, making it a great choice for dogs prone to we3 fatty acids.

Catfish: This freshwater fish is a good source of protein and omega-3 fatty acids. Catfish are also rich in vitamins and minerals such as vitamin B12, niacin, and selenium.

Cod: This white fish is a good source of protein and contains omega-3 fatty acids. Cod is also rich in vitamins B12 and B6, niacin, and phosphorus.

Whiting: This white fish is similar to cod and is a good source of protein and omega-3 fatty acids. Whiting is also rich in vitamins B12 and B6, niacin, and phosphorus.

It's important to note that some fish may contain high levels of mercury, which can be toxic to dogs in large amounts. Always choose fish low in mercury, such as salmon, flounder, and whitefish. Avoid giving your dog raw fish, which may contain harmful bacteria or parasites. You should also remove any bones from cooked fish before feeding it to your dog to avoid choking or other digestive issues.

SUPPLEMENTS

Various supplements can benefit a dog's health depending on their specific needs. Some of the most common supplements include multivitamins, fatty acids, joint supplements, fiber, and probiotics. Let's discuss these in more detail.

CALCIUM SUPPLEMENTATION

If the dog's diet doesn't include raw meaty bones, supplement it with calcium to support healthy bones and teeth. Calcium supplements should be used cautiously in dogs with heart or kidney disease or those receiving digoxin or calcitriol.

The use of calcium supplements during pregnancy or in nursing dogs has not been specifically studied. Still, it is generally considered safe when used in proper doses and under the guidance of your veterinarian.

Before administering any calcium supplements to your dog, it is essential to consult your veterinarian.

MULTIVITAMINS

Multivitamins for dogs can provide essential nutrients such as Vitamin A, C, D, E, K, and B vitamins, which are crucial for maintaining overall health. It's important to remember that human multivitamins should not be given to dogs; instead, ask your veterinarian for product recommendations tailored to your dog's needs.

FATTY ACIDS

Fatty acids, particularly omega-3 and omega-6 fatty acids, are essential for maintaining healthy skin and coat, supporting the immune system, and reducing inflammation. In addition, the body cannot produce these fatty acids, which must be obtained through diet or supplementation.

JOINT SUPPLEMENTS

Joint supplements are commonly used to address joint and mobility issues in dogs, especially seniors or breed prone to joint problems. These supplements often contain ingredients like glucosamine, chondroitin and MSM, which can help improve joint health, reduce pain, and increase mobility.

FIBER SUPPLEMENTS

Fiber Supplements can benefit dogs with digestive issues as they help regulate bowel movements and maintain gastrointestinal health. Fiber can be found in various natural sources like pumpkin or provided as a supplement recommended by your veterinarian.

PROBIOTICS

Probiotics are beneficial bacteria that help support a healthy gut microbiome, which can improve digestion, boost the immune system and promote overall well-being. Probiotic supplements can be helpful for dogs recovering from illness or antibiotic treatments, as well as those with sensitive stomachs or chronic digestive issues. It's key to consult your veterinarian before starting any supplement regimen for your dog,

as their needs will vary based on their diet, lifestyle and health conditions.

THE IMPACT OF DIET ON YOUR DOG'S HEALTH

IMPROVED DIGESTION

One of the most significant benefits of feeding your dog healthy fresh food is improved digestion. Fresh foods contain natural enzymes that aid digestion, resulting in fewer digestive issues and healthier gut flora. This can be especially beneficial for dogs with sensitive stomachs or digestive issues.

Feeding your dog, a wholesome unprocessed diet can improve their digestion and overall health. It can provide a more natural source of nutrients that can be easier for your dog to digest than highly processed kibble or canned foods.

Here are some ways a fresh food diet can improve digestion for dogs:

- Increased moisture content: Fresh food diets typically have a higher moisture content than kibble, which can help keep your dog hydrated and promote healthy digestion. Adequate hydration is important for the overall health of your dog's digestive tract.
- High-quality protein: Natural home-made diets often contain higher-quality proteins from sources like whole meats or fish, which can be easier for dogs to digest and utilize for muscle growth and repair.
- Whole food ingredients: Fresh food diets are often made with whole food ingredients like vegetables and fruits, which provide a source of fiber that can aid digestion and promote healthy bowel movements.
- Limited additives and preservatives: Many commercial dog foods contain additives and preservatives that can be difficult for dogs to digest. Homemade unprocessed diets have no preservatives or additives, which can be easier on your dog's digestive system.
- Customization: With a fresh diet, you can customize your dog's diet based on their needs and preferences. This can help you create a diet tailored to your dog's digestive needs, leading to improved digestion and overall health.
- However, it's important to note that transitioning your dog to a fresh food diet should be done gradually to avoid digestive upset. It's also important to ensure the diet is complete and balanced for your dog's needs. Work with your veterinarian to ensure your dog eats a balanced and complete diet.

ENHANCED IMMUNE SYSTEM

- Fresh ingredients in dog food can enhance a dog's immune system in several ways. First, fresh fruits and vegetables are rich in vitamins, minerals, and antioxidants that can help support a strong immune system.
- Antioxidants, such as vitamin C and vitamin E, can help protect cells from damage caused by free radicals and oxidative stress, which can weaken the immune system.
- Incorporating fresh produce like blueberries, spinach, and sweet potatoes into a dog's diet can give them a rich source of antioxidants and help support their immune system.
- In addition, natural ingredients in dog food can also support gut health, which is closely linked to the immune system. The gut contains many immune cells, and maintaining a healthy balance of gut bacteria is essential for a robust immune system.
- Fresh ingredients, like probiotics, prebiotics, and fiber, can help promote the growth of beneficial gut bacteria and support a healthy immune system.
- Highly processed dog foods can contain artificial colors, flavors, and preservatives that can be difficult for dogs to digest and may negatively impact their immune system over time.
- You can help support your dog's immune systems and promote their overall health and well-being by feeding them a healthy and balanced diet made with fresh, whole ingredients.

HEALTHIER SKIN AND COAT

- Healthy skin and a shiny coat are signs of a dog's overall well-being. Cooking up nutritious meals with natural unprocessed ingredients can promote healthy skin and coat through their protein content, fatty acids, vitamins and minerals, hydration and the avoidance of harmful additives and preservatives. By incorporating fresh wholesome ingredients in your dog's diet, you can promote a thick shiny coat and overall health.

INCREASED ENERGY LEVELS

- Fresh foods are more easily absorbed and utilized by your dog's body, increasing energy levels and vitality. Feeding dogs, a fresh diet can increase energy levels and various health benefits.
- Fiber, a form of carbohydrate, is essential for a dog's gastrointestinal function and health, as it maintains the health of the colon and gut microbes. A new diet of natural, real ingredients like beef, chicken, lamb, peas, spinach, carrots, and blueberries can significantly improve a dog's overall well-being and promote heart health.
- A well-balanced diet should also include appropriate amounts of minerals, vitamins, essential amino acids from proteins, and specific essential fatty acids from fats to support the dog's health and energy levels. By providing a wholesome diet with the right balance of nutrients, dogs can experience increased energy levels and overall better health.
- By providing your dog with a balanced nutritious diet, you can help keep them active and engaged and ensure they get the nutrition they need to thrive.

WEIGHT MANAGEMENT

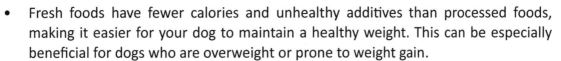

- Fresh foods have fewer calories and unhealthy additives than processed foods, making it easier for your dog to maintain a healthy weight. This can be especially beneficial for dogs who are overweight or prone to weight gain.
- Weight management for dogs on a fresh food diet involves providing appropriate

caloric intake, balancing nutrients, and ensuring proper exercise. In addition, a fresh food diet should cater to the specific energy requirements of dogs, which can vary depending on factors such as age, breed, size, activity level, and overall health.

- Most adult, indoor, spayed, or neutered dogs have relatively low energy requirements. Therefore, their diet should contain fewer calories per cup (ideally less than 350 calories) to prevent overfeeding and weight gain.
- One way to calculate your dog's caloric needs is by using the Resting Energy Requirement (RER formula). Take your dog's weight in kilograms, multiply by 30, and add 70. However, it's important to remember that these calculations are only rough estimates, and your pet's caloric needs can change with time and circumstances.

IDEAL BODY WEIGHT

- Once your dog reaches their ideal body weight, it is important to adjust their feeding schedule to maintain that weight. Dividing their daily caloric intake into two meals per day can help prevent overeating and ensure a balanced diet.
- In conclusion, working closely with your veterinarian to determine your dog's caloric needs is crucial for their overall health and well-being. Monitoring your dog's weight and adjusting their feeding schedule will help them maintain their ideal body weight and lead a happy, healthy life.
- When formulating a fresh healthy nutritious diet, evaluating the nutritional balance, including appropriate amounts of essential nutrients such as proteins, fats, carbohydrates, vitamins, and minerals, is crucial.

CHAPTER 2

UNDERSTANDING KIBBLE AND ITS LIMITATIONS

THE DOWNSIDES OF COMMERCIAL DOG FOOD

- A balanced and complete dog food refers to a product that provides all the essential nutrients a dog requires in the right proportions to support its overall health and well-being. According to the Association of American Feed Control Officials (AAFCO), there are six essential nutrients required to support life and function in dogs. These nutrients include water, carbohydrates (including fiber), vitamins, minerals, fat, and protein. A balanced dog food should meet a dog's energy requirements, which can vary depending on various factors such as age, breed, size, activity level, and overall health. The American Kennel Club (AKC) suggests focusing on the four essential nutrients: protein, fat, fiber, and water.
- Although most commercial dog foods fall within the acceptable range set by the AAFCO, some dog foods can be better for your dog than others, depending on the quality of the ingredients. Here's the takeaway on low-quality commercial dog food.

CANNED DOG FOOD

Low-quality canned dog food can contain ingredients that may not provide optimal nutrition for your dog and could lead to health issues.

Domestic dogs can derive nutrients not only from meat but also from grains, fruits, and vegetables. However, low-quality canned dog food may use ingredients that are less beneficial or may include fillers and artificial additives. It may not meet the minimum nutrient requirements or may contain excessive amounts of certain nutrients, leading to imbalances that could negatively affect your dog's health.

RENDERED INGREDIENTS

Rendered ingredients in low-quality dog kibble and canned foods can harm your dog's health due to their potentially substandard nutritional content and questionable sources.

Rendered ingredients often come from meat or animal by- products cooked and processed to remove moisture and fat, leaving a concentrated protein source.

Low-quality dog kibble typically starts with ground yellow corn or similar cereal grains, followed by a meat or rendered product, such as a poultry by-product meal, which is blended to make a dough.

Rendered ingredients in low-quality kibble can be sourced from lower-grade animal products containing antibiotics, hormones, or traces of euthanasia drugs, which can negatively impact your dog's health.

Canned food, although usually more palatable than dry food, may also contain rendered ingredients that can harm your dog's health if poor quality.

You can take control of the ingredients in your dog's diet by using only unprocessed, natural ingredients in the meals you create for them.

CARBS

Pet obesity is a growing concern, with a survey of veterinary professionals suggesting that around 51% of dogs and 44% of cats are overweight or obese. High carbohydrate content in commercial pet food, especially with added sugars, can contribute to excessive calorie intake, leading to weight gain and obesity. Obesity can, in turn, increase the risk of various health issues such as diabetes, heart disease, and joint problems in pets.

NUTRIENT LOSS

The processing methods used in commercial pet food production can lead to the loss of essential nutrients. The heating process typically destroys one-third to one-half of vitamins A, C, and some B vitamins, depending on the canned food.

PRESERVATIVES AND ARTIFICIAL INGREDIENTS

Preservatives and artificial ingredients play a significant role in commercial dog food, primarily to extend shelf life, maintain freshness, and enhance the appearance and flavor of the food. These ingredients are not beneficial and, in fact, may be harmful to your pup.

CHAPTER 3

INFLAMMATION AND YOUR DOG'S DIET

Low-quality dog food can trigger inflammation in your dog's tissues, leading to various health issues such as joint pain, skin problems, gastrointestinal issues, and a weakened immune system. Dogs require a balanced intake of Omega-6 and Omega-3 fatty acids, as they cannot produce these fats independently. Omega-3s help reduce the inflammatory response, while Omega-6 fats promote it. An imbalance in these fats can contribute to inflammation.

To prevent or manage chronic inflammation, providing your pup with a healthy diet that includes fresh, whole foods rich in antioxidants is the key. Inflammatory vegetables like nightshades (potatoes, tomatoes, eggplant, and peppers) should be avoided.

KIBBLE DIETS

Kibble diets are often in carbohydrates, leading to elevated blood sugar levels and an overactive immune response.

Kibble is typically processed at high temperatures, which can destroy beneficial nutrients and alter the protein structure, which contributes to inflammation and oxidative stress in the body.

OBESITY

Obesity is another factor that can contribute to inflammation in dogs, as excess body fat can release inflammatory chemicals in the body. Therefore, feeding your dog a balanced, nutrient-dense diet that meets their caloric needs and promotes a healthy body weight is essential.

ENDOCRINE DISRUPTING CHEMICALS

Finally, endocrine-disrupting chemicals and pesticides in dog food can also contribute to inflammation in the body. These chemicals have been linked to a range of health issues in both humans and animals, including reproductive disorders and cancer.

These can be avoided when you control the ingredients in your dog's meals.

In conclusion, inflammation is a complex process that various factors, including diet, can influence. Creating high-quality meals rich in beneficial nutrients and free from harmful chemicals and additives can help reduce inflammation and promote overall health and well-being in your dog.

CHAPTER 4

TRANSITIONING FROM KIBBLE TO FRESH DOG FOOD

TRANSITIONING FROM KIBBLE TO FRESH DOG FOOD

Transitioning from kibble to fresh dog food can be an excellent choice for pet owners concerned about the quality of ingredients in commercial dog food.

However, it is important to approach the transition slowly and carefully, considering the dog's digestive system and microbiome. The microbiome is the collection of microorganisms that live in and on a dog's body, including in the digestive tract.

When transitioning to a fresh diet, it is important to give the body time to adapt to a different nutrient blend and ingredients, as the bacteria in the gut will have to change to accommodate and help digest these new nutrients.

GRADUAL STEPS TO INTRODUCE FRESH FOOD INTO YOUR DOG'S DIET

Introducing fresh food into your dog's diet can benefit their health, but it's a good idea to do it gradually to avoid digestive upset. Here are some gradual steps to help you introduce fresh food into your dog's diet:

Start by selecting high-quality, dog-friendly fresh foods: Some good options include organ meats like chicken and beef hearts, which are rich in B vitamins, phosphorus, and essential fatty acids. You can also choose good sources of fiber, like carrots, pumpkins, apples, dark leafy greens, brown rice, and flax seeds. These are all featured in our recipes.

Begin with a small portion: To start, reduce the total amount of processed dog food by 20%, leaving room for fresh additions.

Introduce one fresh food item at a time: Gradually add the new fresh food item to your dog's diet, starting with a small amount, and observe their reaction. This will help you identify any potential allergies or intolerances.

Mix the fresh food with your dog's kibble: For example, add some of your homemade dog food goodness to your dog's kibble and mix it in. This will help your dog become familiar with the taste and texture of the new food.

Monitor your dog's health: Keep an eye on your dog's overall health, coat condition, and energy levels as you introduce fresh foods. If you notice any adverse reactions, discontinue the fresh food item and consult your veterinarian.

Gradually increase the amount of fresh food: As your dog becomes accustomed to the new food, you can gradually increase the amount of fresh food in their diet.

Always consult your veterinarian before significantly changing your dog's diet to ensure you provide the proper nutrients for their needs.

TIPS FOR MAKING THE TRANSITION SMOOTH AND STRESS- FREE

Transitioning your dog from kibble to a fresh food diet can be a smooth and stress-free process if you follow these tips:

- Plan a gradual transition: A typical transition to a new diet should take about seven days, giving your dog's body and gut bacteria time to adapt to the new nutrient blend and ingredients.
- Follow a transition schedule: Mix the fresh food with your dog's kibble during the first few days, gradually increasing the proportion of fresh food while reducing the kibble. A suggested transition schedule is as follows:
- Days 1-3: Feed 25% fresh food and 75% kibble
- Days 4-6: Feed 50% fresh food and 50% kibble
- Days 7-9: Feed 75% fresh food and 25% kibble
- Day 10: You can feed 100% fresh food

Please note that not all dogs transition at the same rate, and some may require a longer or shorter transition period.

- Monitor your dog's health: Keep a close eye on your dog's overall health, energy levels, and digestion during the transition. If you notice any adverse reactions, consult your veterinarian.

Be patient: Some dogs may take longer to adjust to the new diet. Be patient and give your dog the time to adapt to the fresh food.

Consult your veterinarian: Before making any significant changes to your dog's

diet, consult your veterinarian to ensure you're providing the proper nutrients for their

specific needs and to discuss any concerns you may have during the transition process.

By following these tips, you can transition from kibble to a fresh food diet that is smooth and stress-free for you and your dog.

CHAPTER 5

WHAT TO INCLUDE IN YOUR DOG'S DIET AND WHAT TO AVOID

Ensuring a balanced and nutritious diet for our furry friends is essential for their overall health and well-being. Homemade diets for dogs have become increasingly popular.

While they offer a wide range of benefits, such as diet management, appeasing picky eaters, and bond-building, it is important to be cautious in selecting the right ingredients to avoid potential health risks.

It's also key to ensure you feed all the necessary nutrients to keep them healthy and active.

IDENTIFYING UNSAFE INGREDIENTS

When home cooking for dogs, it is crucial to be aware of potentially harmful ingredients that may threaten your pet's health. Some common household foods can cause severe dog health problems and should be avoided. Here's the takeaway:

- Onions and onion powder: These can cause damage to red blood cells, leading to anemia and other complications.
- Grapes and raisins: These can cause kidney failure in dogs.
- Chocolate: It contains Theobromine, which can cause heart problems, tremors, seizures, and even death in dogs.
- Xylitol: Found in many sugar-free products like candy, gum, and toothpaste, xylitol can cause a rapid drop in blood sugar levels, leading to seizures and liver failure.
- Caffeine: Present in coffee, tea, and some other beverages, caffeine can cause heart problems, tremors, and seizures in dogs.
- Macadamia nuts: These can cause weakness, vomiting, tremors, and hyperthermia in dogs.
- Tomato and potato leaves and stems can cause gastrointestinal and nervous system problems.
- Avocados: contain persin, a toxin that can cause diarrhea and vomiting and can be deadly. Avocados are also high in fat, which can lead to pancreatitis in dogs.

- Alcohol: It can cause vomiting, diarrhea, coordination problems, difficulty breathing, coma, and even death in dogs.

Always double-check the ingredients when preparing home-cooked meals for your dogs to ensure their safety and well-being.

ENSURING BALANCED MEALS FOR YOUR DOG

Just like humans, dogs require diverse nutrients to stay healthy. However, the nutrient requirements for dogs can vary based on age, size, breed, and activity level.

Nutrient diversity refers to consuming various foods to obtain all the necessary nutrients in appropriate amounts. This approach ensures that dogs receive all the essential vitamins, minerals, and macronutrients necessary for optimal health.

Incorporating nutrient diversity in your dog's diet is crucial to prevent nutritional deficiencies, which can lead to health problems. For example, a lack of protein can result in muscle atrophy and weakness, while a lack of essential fatty acids can cause dry, itchy skin and a dull coat.

Additionally, insufficient specific vitamins and minerals can lead to more serious health concerns, such as anemia and bone disease. A balanced diet includes a variety of ingredients that provide essential nutrients, such as proteins, carbohydrates, fats, vitamins, and minerals, to support your dog's overall health.

Protein is a vital component of your dog's diet, as it helps with growth and maintenance.

Carbohydrates provide energy and can be found in brown rice, potatoes, and oats. Fiber, a type of carbohydrate, is essential for a healthy digestive system.

Good sources of fiber for dogs include carrots, pumpkins, apples, dark leafy greens, brown rice, and flaxseed. Fats are essential for maintaining healthy skin and coat and providing energy. Dogs require a balance of omega-3 and omega-6 fatty acids which can be obtained from fish oil, flaxseed, and poultry fat.

Vitamins and minerals are required for growth and maintenance, and deficiencies can lead to health problems. For example, dogs need vitamins like A, D, E, and K and minerals like calcium, phosphorus, and potassium, found in fruits, vegetables, and other ingredients.

When preparing homemade dog food, it's essential to include a variety of ingredients that provide the necessary nutrients for a balanced diet.

ESSENTIAL NUTRIENTS FOR YOUR DOG'S HEALTH

Longevity foods (which help lead to a longer healthier life) refer to foods rich in nutrients and provide health benefits for your dog. These foods include leafy greens, sweet potatoes, berries, and fatty fish like salmon. Leafy greens are high in vitamins and minerals, including calcium, iron, and vitamins A, C, and K.

Sweet potatoes are high in fiber and vitamins A and C, which support healthy eyes, skin, and immune systems. Berries are high in antioxidants, which can help reduce inflammation and improve cognitive function. Fatty fish, like salmon, contain omega-3 fatty acids that can help support heart health and reduce inflammation.

CHAPTER 6

DELICIOUS AND NUTRITIOUS DOG FOOD RECIPES

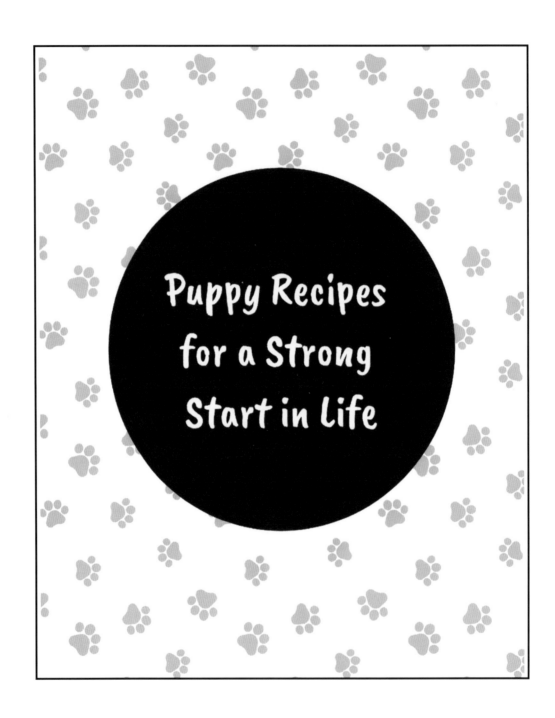

Puppy Recipes
for a Strong
Start in Life

BROWN RICE WITH TURKEY & SPINACH

SERVINGS: 4
PREPPING TIME: 10 MIN
COOKING TIME: 20 MIN

INGREDIENTS

1 lb (454 g) ground turkey
1/4 cups (140 g) fresh spinach, chopped
3/8 cup (75 g) uncooked brown rice
1 small yam, chopped
1/2 tbsp olive oil
3/8 cup (90 ml) low sodium chicken stock

DIRECTIONS

1. Cook the brown rice according to the package instructions. Set aside.
2. Heat the oil in a large soup pot, and brown the ground turkey.
3. Stir in the veggies and chicken stock, and cook for 15 minutes.
4. Add the cooked rice, mix well to combine, and allow to cool.
5. Store 1 week's meals in an airtight container in the fridge and freeze the rest.

NOTES

(254 kcal per 1/2 cup)

CHICKEN AND OATMEAL PUPPY'S BREAKFAST

SERVINGS: 2
PREPPING TIME: 10 MIN
COOKING TIME: 00 MIN

INGREDIENTS

1 cup (80 g) cooked oatmeal
1/2 cup (50 g) cooked, shredded chicken breast
1/4 cup (25 g) chopped apple
1/4 cup (60 g) plain yogurt

DIRECTIONS

1. Mix the cooked oatmeal, shredded chicken breast, chopped apple, and plain yogurt in a small bowl.
2. Divide the mixture between two bowls and serve to your puppy while warm.

NOTES

(150 kcal per serving)

SALMON AND SWEET POTATO CAKES

SERVINGS: 6
PREPPING TIME: 10 MIN
COOKING TIME: 25 MIN

INGREDIENTS

2 cups (400 g) cooked sweet potatoes, mashed
6 oz (170 g) of canned salmon, drained and flaked
1/4 cup (30 g) almond flour
1 egg, beaten

DIRECTIONS

1. Preheat oven to 375°F (190°C).
2. Mix the cooked sweet potatoes, canned salmon, almond flour, and egg in a large bowl until well combined.
3. Form the mixture into six patties.
4. Place the patties on a baking sheet and bake for 25 minutes or until golden brown and cooked through.
5. Let it cool, and serve your puppy.

NOTES

(170 kcal per serving)

CHICKEN AND APPLE BITES

SERVINGS: 6
PREPPING TIME: 10 MIN
COOKING TIME: 25 MIN

INGREDIENTS

17.6 oz (500 g) boneless, skinless chicken breast cut
into small cubes
14 oz (400 g) apples, peeled and cut into small cubes
1/4 cup (60 ml) chicken broth

DIRECTIONS

1. Preheat oven to 375°F (190°C).
2. Mix the chicken cubes, apple cubes, and broth in a bowl until well combined.
3. Spread the mixture evenly on a baking sheet lined with parchment paper.
4. Bake for 20-25 minutes or until the chicken is cooked and the apples tender.
5. Let the bites cool before serving your puppy.

NOTES

(150 kcal per serving)

LAMB AND BARLEY

SERVINGS: 4
PREPPING TIME: 10 MIN
COOKING TIME: 40 MIN

INGREDIENTS

1 lb (450 g) ground lamb
1/2 cup (90 g) barley
1 cup (240 ml) water

DIRECTIONS

1. Rinse the barley thoroughly and soak it in water for 1 hour.
2. In a pot, bring 1 cup of water to a boil and add the soaked barley. Reduce the heat and simmer for 30-40 minutes or until the barley is tender.
3. In a separate pan, cook the ground lamb over medium heat until browned and fully cooked.
4. Drain any excess fat from the lamb.
5. Combine the cooked lamb and barley in a bowl and mix well.
6. Allow the mixture to cool before serving your puppy.

NOTES

(267 kcal per 1/2 cup)

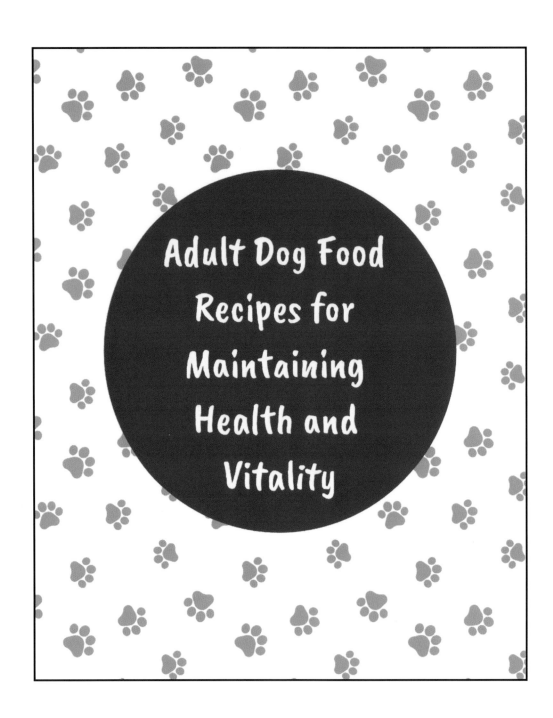

Adult Dog Food Recipes for Maintaining Health and Vitality

LAMB & COUSCOUS

SERVINGS: 6-8
PREPPING TIME: 10 MIN
COOKING TIME: 20 MIN

INGREDIENTS

1 lb (450 g) lamb meat, cut into bite-sized pieces
1 cup (173 g) couscous
1 cup (128 g) chopped carrots
1 cup (125 g) chopped green beans
1/2 cup (30 g) chopped parsley
2 tbsp (30 ml) olive oil
3 cups (750 ml) water

DIRECTIONS

1. In a large pot, heat the olive oil over medium heat.
2. Add the meat and cook until browned, stirring occasionally.
3. Add the chopped carrots and green beans and cook for 5 minutes.
4. Add the couscous and water and bring to a boil.
5. Reduce heat to low, cover, and simmer for 10 minutes.
6. Stir in the chopped parsley and let the mixture cool before serving to your dog.

NOTES

(300 kcal per serving)

LENTIL AND CHICKEN STEW

SERVINGS: 6
PREPPING TIME: 10 MIN
COOKING TIME: 25 MIN

INGREDIENTS

1 cup (200 g) of lentils
1 pound (450 g) of boneless, skinless chicken breasts
cut into small pieces
1 cup (240 ml) chopped carrots
1 cup (240 ml) chopped green beans
1/2 cup (120 ml) chopped celery
4 cups (960 ml) low-sodium chicken broth
2 tablespoons (30 ml) olive oil

DIRECTIONS

1. Rinse the lentils in a large pot with the chicken broth. Bring to a boil and then reduce the heat to low. Simmer for 20-30 minutes or until the lentils are tender.
2. In a separate pan, heat the olive oil over medium heat. Add the chicken pieces and cook until the chicken is no longer pink.
3. Add the cooked chicken, carrots, green beans, and celery to the lentil pot. Simmer for 10-15 minutes or until the vegetables are tender.
4. Allow the stew to cool before serving.

NOTES

(325 kcal per serving)

BAKED COD AND EGG CASSEROLE

SERVINGS: 4-6
PREPPING TIME: 10 MIN
COOKING TIME: 30 MIN

INGREDIENTS

1 lb (450 g) cod fillets, chopped into small pieces
4 eggs
1 cup (30 g) chopped spinach
1/2 cup (85 g) grated carrots
1/2 cup (30 g) chopped parsley
1 tbsp (15 ml) olive oil

DIRECTIONS

1. Preheat the oven to 375°F.
2. In a large bowl, whisk together the eggs and olive oil.
3. Add the chopped cod, spinach, grated carrots, and chopped parsley to the bowl and stir to combine.
4. Pour the mixture into a greased baking dish and smooth out the top.
5. Bake the casserole in the oven for 25-30 minutes or until the top is golden brown and the eggs are cooked.
6. Let the casserole cool to room temperature before serving to your dog.

NOTES

(200 kcal per serving)

SPLIT PEA AND CHICKEN STEW

SERVINGS: 6
PREPPING TIME: 10 MIN
COOKING TIME: 45 MIN

INGREDIENTS

1 pound (450 g) of boneless, skinless chicken breasts
cut into small pieces
1 cup (200 g) split peas, rinsed
2 carrots, chopped
2 celery stalks, chopped
1 sweet potato, peeled and chopped
4 cups (960 ml) low-sodium chicken broth
1 tablespoon (15 ml) olive oil

DIRECTIONS

1. In a large pot, heat the olive oil over medium heat.
2. Add the chicken pieces and cook until browned on all sides.
3. Add the split peas, carrots, celery, sweet potato, and chicken broth to the pot.
4. Bring the mixture to a boil, then reduce the heat and simmer for 45-60 minutes, or until the vegetables and split peas are tender.
5. Allow the stew to cool before serving.

NOTES

(250 kcal per serving)

PORK AND GREEN BEAN CASSEROLE

SERVINGS: 4-6
PREPPING TIME: 10 MIN
COOKING TIME: 30 MIN

INGREDIENTS

1 lb (450 g) ground pork
2 cups (250 g) of green beans, trimmed and chopped
2 cups (380 g) of brown rice
2 cups (500 ml) of water
1 tablespoon (15 ml) of olive oil

DIRECTIONS

1. Cook the ground pork over medium heat until it's browned.
2. Add the green beans, brown rice, water, and olive oil to the pan with the pork.
3. Bring the mixture to a boil, reduce the heat to low, and cover the pan.
4. Simmer the mixture for 25-30 minutes or until the rice is fully cooked.
5. Allow the mixture to cool before serving it to your dog.

NOTES

(460 kcal per cup)

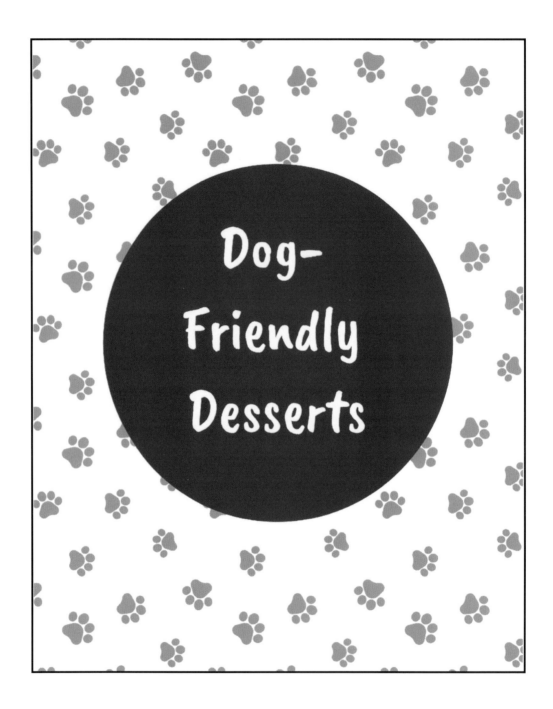

Dog-
Friendly
Desserts

BANANA & PEANUT BUTTER CREPES

SERVINGS: 4-6
PREPPING TIME: 10 MIN
COOKING TIME: 12 MIN

INGREDIENTS

1/2 cup (60 g) whole wheat flour
1/2 cup (120 ml) water
1 egg
1 tablespoon (15 ml) coconut oil, melted
1/4 cup (60 g) unsweetened peanut butter
1 medium banana, sliced

DIRECTIONS

1. Whisk together whole wheat flour, water, egg, and melted coconut oil in a mixing bowl to create a smooth batter.
2. Heat a non-stick skillet over medium heat.
3. Pour about 1/4 cup (60ml) of the batter onto the skillet and spread it thinly into a circle.
4. Cook the crepe for 2 minutes on each side or until golden brown. Repeat with the remaining batter to make additional crepes.
5. Spread a thin layer of unsweetened peanut butter on each crepe and top with banana slices.
6. Fold the crepes in half and serve.

NOTES

(80 kcal per crepe)

APPLE & CARROT PUP CAKES

SERVINGS: 10-12
PREPPING TIME: 10 MIN
COOKING TIME: 25 MIN

INGREDIENTS

1 cup (125 g) whole wheat flour
1 teaspoon (4 g) baking powder
1/2 cup (120 ml) unsweetened applesauce
1/4 cup (60 ml) honey
1/4 cup (60 ml) vegetable oil
1 egg
1 cup (128 g) grated carrots

DIRECTIONS

1. Preheat your oven to 350°F (175°C) and line a muffin tin with paper liners or grease with non-stick cooking spray.
2. In a mixing bowl, combine whole wheat flour and baking powder.
3. Whisk together applesauce, honey, vegetable oil, and egg in a separate bowl.
4. Gradually add the wet ingredients to the dry ingredients, mixing until combined.
5. Fold in the grated carrots.
6. Fill each muffin cup about 3/4 full with the batter.
7. Bake for 20-25 minutes or until a toothpick inserted in the center comes clean.
8. Allow the pup cakes to cool before serving.

NOTES

(90 kcal per pup cake)

PUMPKIN & OAT DOG COOKIES

SERVINGS: 18-20
PREPPING TIME: 10 MIN
COOKING TIME: 20 MIN

INGREDIENTS

2 cups (180 g) rolled oats
1 cup (240 g) canned pumpkin puree (unsweetened)
1/4 cup (60 g) unsweetened peanut butter
1/4 cup (60 ml) water

DIRECTIONS

1. Preheat your oven to 350°F (175°C) and line a baking sheet with parchment paper.
2. Combine rolled oats, pumpkin puree, peanut butter, and water in a mixing bowl. Mix until a thick dough forms.
3. Use a cookie scoop or your hands to form small dough balls and place them on the prepared baking sheet.
4. Flatten each ball with a fork or your fingers.
5. Bake for 20-25 minutes or until the cookies are firm and golden brown.
6. Allow the cookies to cool completely before serving.

NOTES

(50 kcal per cookie)

FROZEN BLUEBERRY & YOGURT TREATS

SERVINGS: 12-16
PREPPING TIME: 10 MIN
COOKING TIME: 00 MIN

INGREDIENTS

1 cup (150 g) fresh or frozen blueberries
1 cup (240 g) plain, low-fat yogurt
2 tablespoons (30 ml) honey

DIRECTIONS

1. In a blender, combine blueberries, yogurt, and honey. Blend until smooth.
2. Pour the mixture into ice cube trays or silicone molds.
3. Freeze for at least 4 hours or until completely solid.
4. Remove the frozen treats from the trays or molds and serve. Store any leftovers in an airtight container in the freezer.

NOTES

(20 kcal per treat)

PEANUT BUTTER & BANANA FROZEN BITES

SERVINGS: 12-16
PREPPING TIME: 10 MIN
COOKING TIME: 20 MIN

INGREDIENTS

2 ripe bananas
1/2 cup (120 g) unsweetened peanut butter
1/4 cup (60 ml) unsweetened almond milk

DIRECTIONS

1. Combine bananas, peanut butter, and almond milk in a blender or food processor. Blend until smooth.
2. Pour the mixture into ice cube trays or silicone molds.
3. Freeze for at least 4 hours or until completely solid.
4. Remove the frozen bites from the trays or molds and serve. Store any leftovers in an airtight container in the freezer.

NOTES

(30 kcal per bite)

SWEET POTATO & APPLE CHEWS

SERVINGS: 8-10
PREPPING TIME: 10 MIN
COOKING TIME: 2-3 HRS

INGREDIENTS

1 large sweet potato, peeled and sliced into 1/4-inch (0.6 cm) thick pieces
1 large apple, cored and sliced into 1/4-inch (0.6 cm) wide pieces

DIRECTIONS

1. Preheat your oven to 250°F (120°C) and line a baking sheet with parchment paper.
2. Arrange the sweet potato and apple slices on the prepared baking sheet in a single layer.
3. Bake for 2-3 hours, flipping the slices halfway through until they are dry and chewy.
4. Allow the chews to cool completely before serving. Store leftovers in an airtight container.

NOTES

(40 kcal per chew) The number of servings will depend on the size of the sweet potato and apple used and how many chews are given per serving. However, assuming that each serving is about 1-2 chews.

COCONUT & BERRY DOGGY DONUTS

SERVINGS: 6-8
PREPPING TIME: 10 MIN
COOKING TIME: 15 MIN

INGREDIENTS

1 1/2 cups (180 g) whole wheat flour
1/2 cup (40 g) unsweetened shredded coconut
1 teaspoon (4 g) baking powder
1/2 cup (120 ml) coconut milk
1/4 cup (60 ml) honey
1 egg
1/2 cup (75 g) mixed berries (fresh or frozen)

DIRECTIONS

1. Preheat your oven to 350°F (175°C) and grease a donut pan with non-stick cooking spray.
2. Combine whole wheat flour, shredded coconut, and baking powder in a mixing bowl.
3. Whisk together coconut milk, honey, and egg in a separate bowl.
4. Gradually add the wet ingredients to the dry ingredients, mixing until combined.
5. Fold in the mixed berries.
6. Fill each donut cavity about 3/4 full with the batter.
7. Bake for 15-20 minutes or until a toothpick inserted in the center comes out clean.
8. Allow the donuts to cool before serving.

NOTES

(60 kcal per donut)

CAROB CHIP & OAT COOKIES

SERVINGS: 12
PREPPING TIME: 10 MIN
COOKING TIME: 15 MIN

INGREDIENTS

1 1/2 cups (135 g) rolled oats
1/2 cup (64 g) whole wheat flour
1/2 cup (80 g) carob chips
1/4 cup (60 ml) coconut oil, melted
1/4 cup (60 ml) honey
1 egg

DIRECTIONS

1. Preheat your oven to 350°F (175°C) and line a baking sheet with parchment paper.
2. Combine rolled oats, whole wheat flour, and carob chips in a mixing bowl.
3. Whisk together melted coconut oil, honey, and egg in a separate bowl.
4. Gradually add the wet ingredients to the dry ingredients, mixing until combined.
5. Use a cookie scoop or your hands to form small dough balls and place them on the prepared baking sheet.
6. Flatten each ball with a fork or your fingers.
7. Bake for 12-15 minutes or until the cookies are firm and golden brown.
8. Allow the cookies to cool completely before serving.

NOTES

(45 kcal per cookie)

STRAWBERRY & COTTAGE CHEESE PARFAIT

SERVINGS: 2-4
PREPPING TIME: 10 MIN
COOKING TIME: 00 MIN

INGREDIENTS

1 cup (150 g) fresh strawberries, sliced
1 cup (225 g) low-fat cottage cheese
1 tablespoon (15 ml) honey
1/4 cup (20 g) unsweetened shredded coconut

DIRECTIONS

1. In a small bowl, mix the cottage cheese and honey.
2. Layer the strawberry slices, sweetened cottage cheese, and shredded coconut in a glass or bowl.
3. Repeat the layers until all the ingredients are used.
4. Serve immediately or refrigerate until ready to serve.

NOTES

(50 kcal per serving)

Fresh Dog Food Recipes for Overweight Dogs

VENISON & CARROT STEW

SERVINGS: 4-6
PREPPING TIME: 15 MIN
COOKING TIME: 6 HRS

INGREDIENTS

400 g (14 oz) venison stew meat, cubed
1 large sweet potato (approx. 250 g), peeled and cubed
1 cup (150 g) chopped carrots
1/2 cup (120 ml) low-sodium beef broth
1 tablespoon (15 ml) olive oil
1/2 teaspoon (2 g) dried sage

DIRECTIONS

1. Combine the cubed venison stew meat in a crockpot, cubed sweet potatoes, chopped carrots, low-sodium beef broth, olive oil, and dried sage.
2. Cover the crockpot and cook on low for 6-8 hours or on high for 3-4 hours or until the venison and the vegetables are tender.
3. Allow the stew to cool before serving. Store leftovers in the refrigerator for up to 4 days or freeze them in individual portions.

NOTES

(180 kcal per cup)

DUCK & APPLE STEW

SERVINGS: 4-6
PREPPING TIME: 10 MIN
COOKING TIME: 6 HRS

INGREDIENTS

400g (14 oz) cooked duck breast, shredded
2 cups (300 g) chopped apples
1 cup (150 g) chopped green beans
2 cups (480 ml) low-sodium chicken broth
1 tablespoon (15 ml) coconut oil
1/2 teaspoon (2 g) dried parsley

DIRECTIONS

1. Combine the shredded cooked duck breast, chopped apples, green beans, low-sodium chicken broth, coconut oil, and dried parsley in a crockpot.
2. Cover the crockpot and cook on low for 6-8 hours or on high for 3-4 hours or until the apples are tender.
3. Allow the stew to cool before serving. Store leftovers in the refrigerator for up to 4 days or freeze them in individual portions.

NOTES

(160 kcal per cup)

BEEF & QUINOA STEW

SERVINGS: 4-6
PREPPING TIME: 10 MIN
COOKING TIME: 40 MIN

INGREDIENTS

400 g (14 oz) beef stew meat, cubed
1 cup (150 g) uncooked quinoa
1 cup (150 g) chopped zucchini
1 cup (150 g) chopped carrots
1 cup (150 g) chopped sweet potato
1 cup (150 g) chopped green beans
1 cups (500 ml) low-sodium beef broth
1 tablespoon (15 ml) olive oil
1/2 teaspoon (2 g) dried oregano

DIRECTIONS

1. In a large pot, heat the olive oil over medium heat.
2. Add the cubed beef stew meat and cook until browned on all sides, about 5-7 minutes.
3. Add the chopped zucchini, carrots, sweet potato, and green beans to the pot and stir to combine with the beef.
4. Pour in the low-sodium beef broth and add the dried oregano. Bring the mixture to a boil, then reduce the heat and let it simmer for 15-20 minutes or until the veggies are tender.
5. Add the uncooked quinoa to the pot and stir to combine. Let it simmer for 15-20 minutes or until the quinoa is cooked and the stew thickens.
6. Allow the stew to cool down before serving it to your dog.

NOTES

(300 kcal per cup)

FILET MIGNON & VEGETABLE STEW

SERVINGS: 4-6
PREPPING TIME: 10 MIN
COOKING TIME: 6 HRS

INGREDIENTS

400g (14 oz) filet mignon, cubed
1 cup (150 g) chopped green beans
1 cup (150 g) chopped carrots
1/2 cup (75 g) chopped red bell pepper
2 cups (480 ml) low-sodium beef broth
1/2 teaspoon (2 g) dried thyme

DIRECTIONS

1. Combine the cubed filet mignon, chopped green beans, chopped carrots, chopped red bell pepper, low-sodium beef broth, and dried thyme in a crockpot.
2. Cover the crockpot and cook on low for 6-8 hours or until the beef is cooked and the vegetables are tender.
3. Allow the stew to cool before serving. Store leftovers in the refrigerator for up to 4 days or freeze them in individual portions.

NOTES

(200 kcal per cup)

SALMON & SWEET POTATO CHOWDER

SERVINGS: 4-6
PREPPING TIME: 10 MIN
COOKING TIME: 6 HRS

INGREDIENTS

400 g (14 oz) cooked salmon, flaked
2 large sweet potatoes (approx. 500 g), peeled and cubed
1 cup (150 g) chopped celery
1/2 cup (120 ml) low-sodium chicken broth
1/2 cup (120 ml) coconut milk
1 tablespoon (15 ml) coconut oil
1/2 teaspoon (2 g) dried dill

DIRECTIONS

1. Combine the flaked cooked salmon, cubed sweet potatoes, chopped celery, low-sodium chicken broth, coconut milk, coconut oil, and dried dill in a crockpot.
2. Cover the crockpot and cook on low for 6-8 hours or on high for 3-4 hours or until the sweet potatoes are tender.
3. Allow the chowder to cool before serving. Store leftovers in the refrigerator for up to 4 days or freeze them in individual portions.

NOTES

(40 kcal per chew)

TURKEY AND VEGETABLE STEW

SERVINGS: 7
PREPPING TIME: 10 MIN
COOKING TIME: 25 MIN

INGREDIENTS

1 lb (450 g) ground turkey
1 cup (195 g) brown rice
1 cup (100 g) chopped green beans
1 cup (128 g) chopped carrots
1 cup (30 g) chopped spinach
4 cups (1000 ml) low-sodium chicken broth

DIRECTIONS

1. In a large pot, cook the ground turkey over medium-high heat until browned.
2. Add the brown rice, green beans, carrots, spinach, and chicken broth.
3. Bring the mixture to a boil and then reduce the heat to low. Cover and simmer for 20-25 minutes or until the rice is tender.
4. Allow the stew to cool before serving. Store leftovers in the refrigerator for up to 4 days or freeze them in individual portions.

NOTES

(181 kcal per cup)

SALMON AND SWEET POTATO PATTIES

SERVINGS: 3-4
PREPPING TIME: 10 MIN
COOKING TIME: 10 MIN

INGREDIENTS

1 14 oz (396 g) can of salmon
1 large sweet potato, peeled and grated
1/4 cup (15 g) chopped parsley
1/4 cup (30 g) coconut flour
1 egg
1 tablespoon (30 ml) coconut oil

DIRECTIONS

Drain the can of salmon and remove any bones or skin. Place the salmon in a mixing bowl.
Add the grated sweet potato, chopped parsley, coconut flour, and egg to the mixing bowl.
Mix everything until well combined.
Form the mixture into patties.
Heat the coconut oil in a large skillet over medium-high heat.
Cook the patties on each side for 3-4 minutes or until golden brown.
Allow the patties to cool before serving. Store leftovers in the refrigerator for up to 4 days
or freeze them in individual portions.

NOTES

(117 kcal per Pattie)

LENTIL AND BEEF MEATBALLS

SERVINGS: 20
PREPPING TIME: 10 MIN
COOKING TIME: 30 MIN

INGREDIENTS

1 cup (200 g) of cooked lentils
1 pound (450 g) of lean ground beef
1/2 cup (120 ml) chopped carrots
1/2 cup (120 ml) chopped spinach
1/4 cup (60 ml) plain Greek yogurt
1 egg
1 teaspoon (5 ml) dried parsley
1 teaspoon (5 ml) dried oregano
1 tablespoon (15 ml) olive oil

DIRECTIONS

1. Preheat the oven to 375°F (190°C).
2. Mix the cooked lentils, ground beef, carrots, spinach, Greek yogurt, egg, parsley, and oregano in a large bowl until well combined.
3. Roll the mixture into small meatballs and place them on a lined baking sheet.
4. Brush the meatballs with olive oil and bake for 25-30 minutes or until cooked.
5. Allow the meatballs to cool before serving.

NOTES

(65 kcal per meatball)

TURKEY AND WINTER SQUASH CASSEROLE

SERVINGS: 4
PREPPING TIME: 15 MIN
COOKING TIME: 25 MIN

INGREDIENTS

1 pound (450 grams) ground turkey
1 cups (480 ml) winter squash, chopped
1 cup (240 ml) green beans, chopped
1/2 cup (120 ml) carrots, chopped
1/4 cup (60 ml) chicken broth
1 tablespoon (15 ml) olive oil
1/4 cup (30 g) grated Parmesan cheese (optional)

DIRECTIONS

1. Preheat oven to 375°F (190°C).
2. Mix the ground turkey, winter squash, green beans, carrots, chicken broth, and olive oil in a large bowl until well combined.
3. Transfer the mixture to a casserole dish and sprinkle the Parmesan cheese.
4. Bake for 20-25 minutes until the casserole is cooked and the cheese is melted.
5. Allow the casserole to cool before serving.

NOTES

(295 kcal per serving)

Fresh Dog
Food Recipes
for Dogs with
Cancer

TURKEY & VEGGIE MEDLEY

SERVINGS: 4
PREPPING TIME: 10 MIN
COOKING TIME: 10 MIN

INGREDIENTS

400 g (14 oz) lean ground turkey
1 cup (150 g) diced zucchini
1 cup (130 g) diced carrots
1/2 cup (75 g) green peas
1/2 cup (80 g) cooked quinoa
1 tablespoon (15 ml) fish oil
1/2 teaspoon (2 g) turmeric powder

DIRECTIONS

1. In a large skillet, cook the ground turkey over medium heat until browned and cooked. Set aside.
2. Steam the zucchini, carrots, and peas until tender. Alternatively, microwave them in a microwave-safe dish with a little water for 5-7 minutes.
3. Combine the cooked turkey, steamed vegetables, cooked quinoa, fish oil, and turmeric powder in a large mixing bowl. Mix well.
4. Allow the mixture to cool before serving. Store leftovers in the refrigerator for up to 4 days or freeze in individual portions.

NOTES

(200 kcal per cup)

CHICKEN & SWEET POTATO STEW

SERVINGS: 2-3
PREPPING TIME: 10 MIN
COOKING TIME: 25 MIN

INGREDIENTS

400 g (14 oz) boneless, skinless chicken breast, diced
1 large sweet potato (approx. 250 g), peeled and cubed
1 cup (100 g) chopped green beans
1 cup (240 ml) low-sodium chicken broth
1 tablespoon (15 ml) flaxseed oil
1/2 teaspoon (2 g) turmeric powder

DIRECTIONS

1. Combine diced chicken, sweet potato cubes, green beans, and low- sodium chicken broth in a large pot.
2. Bring the mixture to a boil, then reduce the heat to low and simmer for 20-25 minutes or until the chicken is cooked through and the sweet potato is tender.
3. Remove the pot from the heat and stir in the flaxseed oil and turmeric powder.
4. Allow the stew to cool before serving. Store leftovers in the refrigerator for up to 4 days or freeze in individual portions.

NOTES

(220 kcal per cup)

FISH & BROWN RICE BOWL

SERVINGS: 4
PREPPING TIME: 10 MIN
COOKING TIME: 10 MIN

INGREDIENTS

400g (14 oz) boneless, skinless white fish (e.g., cod, tilapia), cubed
1 cup (185 g) cooked brown rice
1 cup (150 g) chopped broccoli
1/2 cup (50 g) diced red bell pepper
1 tablespoon (15 ml) fish oil
1/2 teaspoon (2 g) turmeric powder

DIRECTIONS

1. Steam or poach the fish until it's cooked and flakes easily with a fork. Set aside.
2. Steam the broccoli and red bell pepper until tender. Alternatively, microwave them in a microwave-safe dish with a little water for 5-7 minutes.
3. Combine the cooked fish, brown rice, steamed vegetables, fish oil, and turmeric powder in a large mixing bowl. Mix well.
4. Allow the mixture to cool before serving. Store leftovers in the refrigerator for up to 4 days or freeze in individual portions.

NOTES

(180 kcal per cup)

BEEF & PUMPKIN CASSEROLE

SERVINGS: 4
PREPPING TIME: 10 MIN
COOKING TIME: 25 MIN

INGREDIENTS

400g (14 oz) lean ground beef
1 cup (245 g) canned pumpkin puree (unsweetened)
1/2 cup (90 g) cooked lentils
1 cup (70 g) chopped kale
1/4 cup (60 ml) bone broth
1/2 teaspoon (2 g) dried parsley

DIRECTIONS

1. Preheat your oven to 375°F (190°C) and grease a casserole dish with non- stick cooking spray.
2. In a large skillet, cook the ground beef over medium heat until browned and cooked. Set aside.
3. Combine the canned pumpkin puree, cooked lentils, chopped kale, bone broth, and dried parsley in a mixing bowl. Mix well.
4. Add the cooked ground beef to the mixture and stir to combine.
5. Transfer the mixture to the prepared casserole dish and bake for 20-25 minutes or until heated.
6. Allow the casserole to cool before serving. Store leftovers in the refrigerator for up to 4 days or freeze in individual portions.

NOTES

(230 kcal per cup)

LAMB & SPINACH STIR-FRY

SERVINGS: 4
PREPPING TIME: 10 MIN
COOKING TIME: 10 MIN

INGREDIENTS

400 g (14 oz) ground lamb
1 cup (140 g) chopped spinach
1/2 cup (75 g) chopped carrots
1/2 cup (75 g) diced red bell pepper
1 tablespoon (15 ml) coconut oil
1/2 teaspoon (2 g) dried oregano
1/4 teaspoon (1 g) ground cinnamon

DIRECTIONS

1. In a large skillet, heat the coconut oil over medium-high heat.
2. Add the ground lamb and cook until browned, breaking it up into small pieces with a spatula as it cooks.
3. Add the chopped spinach, carrots, diced red bell pepper, dried oregano, and ground cinnamon to the skillet. Stir to combine.
4. Cook for 5-7 minutes or until the vegetables are tender and the lamb is cooked through.
5. Allow the stir-fry to cool before serving. Store leftovers in the refrigerator for up to 4 days or freeze in individual portions.

NOTES

(210 kcal per cup)

BRUSSELS SPROUTS AND BEEF MEATBALLS

SERVINGS: 12-16
PREPPING TIME: 10 MIN
COOKING TIME: 30 MIN

INGREDIENTS

1 pound (450 g) of ground beef
2 cups (480 ml) Brussels sprouts, trimmed and finely chopped
1 medium carrot, peeled and finely grated
1/2 cup (120 ml) low-sodium beef broth
1/4 cup (60 ml) chopped fresh parsley
2 tablespoons (30 ml) olive oil

DIRECTIONS

1. Preheat the oven to 375°F (190°C).
2. Mix the ground beef, Brussels sprouts, carrot, beef broth, and parsley until well combined in a large bowl.
3. Roll the mixture into small meatballs and place them on a lined baking sheet.
4. Drizzle the olive oil over the meatballs.
5. Bake for 20-25 minutes or until the meatballs are cooked through.
6. Allow the meatballs to cool before serving.

NOTES

(50 kcal per meatball)

BEEF & GREEN BEAN STEW

SERVINGS: 3-4
PREPPING TIME: 10 MIN
COOKING TIME: 10 MIN

INGREDIENTS

400 g (14 oz) lean ground beef
1 cup (130 g) chopped green beans
1/2 cup (75 g) diced zucchini
1/2 cup (75 g) diced yellow squash
1/2 teaspoon (2 g) ground cinnamon
1 tablespoon (15 ml) coconut oil

DIRECTIONS

1. In a large skillet, cook the ground beef over medium heat until browned and cooked. Set aside.
2. Steam the green beans, zucchini, and yellow squash until tender. Alternatively, microwave them in a microwave-safe dish with a little water for 5-7 minutes.
3. Combine the cooked ground beef, steamed vegetables, ground cinnamon, and coconut oil in a large mixing bowl. Mix well.
4. Allow the mixture to cool before serving. Store leftovers in the refrigerator for up to 4 days or freeze them in individual portions.

NOTES

(190 kcal per cup)

TURKEY & SWEET POTATO CASSEROLE

SERVINGS: 2-3
PREPPING TIME: 10 MIN
COOKING TIME: 10 MIN

INGREDIENTS

400 g (14 oz) lean ground turkey
1 large sweet potato (approx. 250 g), peeled and cubed
1 cup (130 g) chopped broccoli
1/2 cup (120 ml) low-sodium chicken broth
1 tablespoon (15 ml) olive oil

DIRECTIONS

1. Preheat your oven to 375°F (190°C) and grease a casserole dish with non- stick cooking spray.
2. In a large skillet, cook the ground turkey over medium heat until browned and cooked. Set aside.
3. Steam the sweet potato and broccoli until tender. Alternatively, microwave them in a microwave-safe dish with a little water for 5-7 minutes.
4. Combine the cooked ground turkey, steamed sweet potato and broccoli, low-sodium chicken broth, and olive oil in a mixing bowl. Mix well.
5. Transfer the mixture to the prepared casserole dish and bake for 20-25 minutes or until heated.
6. Allow the casserole to cool before serving. Store leftovers in the refrigerator for up to 4 days or freeze them in individual portions.

NOTES

(180 kcal per cup)

CHICKEN & ASPARAGUS STIR-FRY

SERVINGS: 2-3
PREPPING TIME: 10 MIN
COOKING TIME: 10 MIN

INGREDIENTS

400 g (14 oz) boneless, skinless chicken breast, diced
1 cup (140 g) chopped asparagus
1/2 cup (75 g) diced carrots
1/2 cup (75 g) diced celery
1 tablespoon (15 ml) sesame oil
1/2 teaspoon (2 g) ground ginger

DIRECTIONS

1. In a large skillet, heat the sesame oil over medium-high heat.
2. Add the diced chicken and cook until browned and cooked through.
3. Add the chopped asparagus, carrots, celery, and ground ginger to the skillet. Stir to combine.
4. Cook for 5-7 minutes or until the vegetables are tender.
5. Allow the stir-fry to cool before serving. Store leftovers in the refrigerator for up to 4 days or freeze them in individual portions.

NOTES

(170 kcal per cup)

TURKEY & SPINACH MEATBALLS

SERVINGS: 12-16
PREPPING TIME: 10 MIN
COOKING TIME: 25 MIN

INGREDIENTS

400 g (14 oz) lean ground turkey
1 cup (30 g) chopped spinach
1/2 cup (50 g) grated low-fat Parmesan cheese
1 egg
1/2 teaspoon (2 g) dried oregano

DIRECTIONS

1. Preheat your oven to 375°F (190°C) and line a baking sheet with parchment paper.
2. Combine the ground turkey, chopped spinach, grated Parmesan cheese, egg, and dried oregano in a mixing bowl. Mix well.
3. Use a cookie scoop or your hands to form small meatballs and place them on the prepared baking sheet.
4. Bake for 20-25 minutes or until the meatballs are browned and cooked.
5. Allow the meatballs to cool before serving. Store leftovers in the refrigerator for up to 4 days or freeze them in individual portions.

NOTES

(180 kcal per cup)

BEEF AND BARLEY STEW

SERVINGS: 4
PREPPING TIME: 10 MIN
COOKING TIME: 35 MIN

INGREDIENTS

1 pound (450 g) of lean ground beef
1 cup (190 g) of barley
1 cup (240 ml) green beans, chopped
1/2 cup (120 ml) carrots, chopped
1/2 cup (120 ml) frozen peas
1/4 cup (60 ml) low-sodium beef broth
1 tablespoon (15 ml) olive oil

DIRECTIONS

1.   In a large pot, heat the olive oil over medium heat.
2.   Add the ground beef and cook until browned.
3.   Add the barley, green beans, carrots, peas, and beef broth to the pot.
4.   Bring the mixture to a boil, then reduce the heat and simmer for 30-40 minutes or until the barley is tender.
5.   Allow the stew to cool before serving.

NOTES

(340 kcal per serving)

CHICKEN AND BARLEY CASSEROLE

SERVINGS: 6
PREPPING TIME: 10 MIN
COOKING TIME: 25 MIN

INGREDIENTS

1 pound (450 g) of boneless, skinless chicken breasts cut into small pieces
1 cup (190 g) of barley
1/2 cup (120 ml) green peas
1/2 cup (120 ml) carrots, chopped
1/2 cup (120 ml) low-sodium chicken broth
1/4 cup (60 ml) water
1 tablespoon (15 ml) olive oil

DIRECTIONS

1.   Preheat oven to 375°F (190°C).
2.   In a large skillet, heat the olive oil over medium heat.
3.   Add the chicken pieces and cook until browned on all sides.
4.   Add the barley, green peas, carrots, chicken broth, and water to the skillet.
5.   Bring the mixture to a boil, then reduce the heat and simmer for 20-25 minutes or until the barley is tender.
6.   Transfer the mixture to a casserole dish and bake for 20-25 minutes or until the top is golden brown.
7.   Allow the casserole to cool before serving.

NOTES

(280 kcal per serving)

Fresh Dog
Food Recipes
for Dogs with
Arthritis

SALMON AND SWEET POTATO MASH

SERVINGS: 4
PREPPING TIME: 10 MIN
COOKING TIME: 25 MIN

INGREDIENTS

1 pound (450 g) skinless salmon fillets
2 large sweet potatoes, peeled and chopped
1/2 cup (120 ml) low-sodium chicken broth
1 tablespoon (15 ml) olive oil
1/4 teaspoon (1.25 ml) ground turmeric
1/4 teaspoon (1.25 ml) ground ginger

DIRECTIONS

1. Preheat oven to 375°F (190°C).
2. Place the salmon fillets on a lined baking sheet and bake for 15-20 minutes or until cooked.
3. While the salmon is cooking, place the sweet potatoes in a large pot and cover them with water.
4. Bring the water to a boil, then reduce the heat and simmer for 20-25 minutes or until the sweet potatoes are tender.
5. Drain the sweet potatoes and mash them with chicken broth, olive oil, turmeric, and ginger.
6. Serve the cooked salmon with a scoop of the sweet potato mash.

NOTES

(300 kcal per serving)

SALMON AND KALE SALAD

SERVINGS: 8-10
PREPPING TIME: 10 MIN
COOKING TIME: 00 MIN

INGREDIENTS

1 lb (454 g) cooked salmon, flaked
2 cups (65 g) kale chopped
1/2 cup (90 g) cooked brown rice
1/4 cup (60 g) plain Greek yogurt

DIRECTIONS

Mix salmon, kale, and brown rice in a large bowl.
Add Greek yogurt and mix until well combined.

NOTES

(213 kcal per 1/2 cup)

SARDINE AND SQUASH MASH

SERVINGS: 1
PREPPING TIME: 10 MIN
COOKING TIME: 15 MIN

INGREDIENTS

1 cup (3.75 oz/106 g) of sardines in water
1/2 cup (120 g) of cooked and mashed squash
1 tbsp (15 ml) of olive oil
1/4 tsp (1.25 ml) of dried parsley

DIRECTIONS

1. Drain the water from the can of sardines.
2. Cook the squash by peeling and removing the seeds, then chopping it into small pieces. Boil or steam the squash until it is tender. Drain the squash and mash it with a fork or potato masher until it is smooth and creamy.
3. Combine the sardines, cooked and mashed squash, olive oil, and parsley in a medium mixing bowl.
4. Mix everything until well combined.
5. Serve the mash to your dog.

NOTES

(160 kcal per serving)

APPLE AND YAM STEW

SERVINGS: 6
PREPPING TIME: 10 MIN
COOKING TIME: 25 MIN

INGREDIENTS

12 oz (340 g) boneless, skinless chicken breasts
1 large yam (about 1 lb /450 g), peeled and chopped
1 medium apple, peeled and chopped
2 cups (300 g) mixed vegetables (carrots, green beans, and peas), chopped
1/2 cup (120 ml) low-sodium chicken broth
1 tbsp (15 ml) olive oil
1/4 tsp (1.25 ml) dried thyme
1/4 tsp (1.25 ml) dried rosemary

DIRECTIONS

Cut the chicken breasts into small pieces and place them in a large pot or Dutch oven.
Add the chopped yam, apple, mixed vegetables, chicken broth, olive oil, thyme, and rosemary to the pot.
Stir everything together and bring the mixture to a boil.
Reduce the heat to low and simmer for 20-25 minutes until the chicken is cooked and the vegetables are tender.
Allow the stew to cool before serving your dog.

NOTES

(190 kcal per serving)

APPLE AND YAM MASH

SERVINGS: 4
PREPPING TIME: 5 MIN
COOKING TIME: 20 MIN

INGREDIENTS

1 lb (450 g) yam, peeled and chopped
1 medium apple, peeled and chopped
1/4 cup (60 ml) low-sodium chicken broth

DIRECTIONS

1. Add the chopped yam and apple to a large pot and cover with water.
2. Bring the pot to a boil and cook for 20-25 minutes or until the yam is tender.
3. Drain the water and mash the yam and apple with a potato masher or fork.
4. Add the chicken broth and mix until well combined.
5. Allow the mash to cool before serving your dog.

NOTES

(110 kcal per serving)

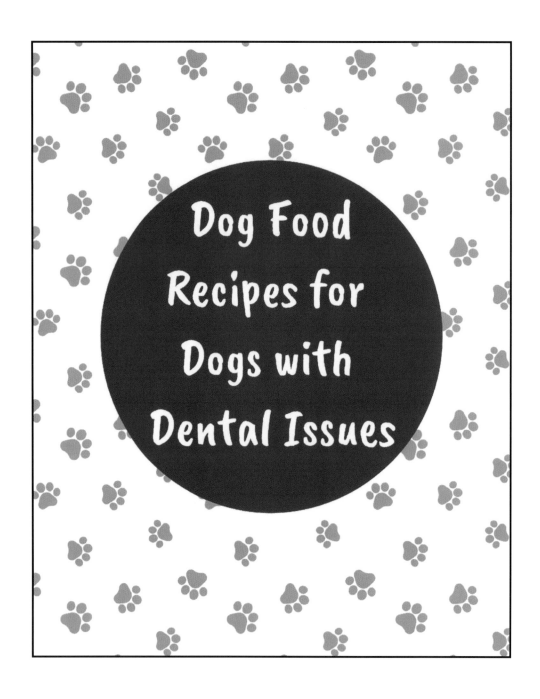

Dog Food Recipes for Dogs with Dental Issues

TURKEY AND VEGETABLE OATMEAL

SERVINGS: 8-10
PREPPING TIME: 10 MIN
COOKING TIME: 10 MIN

INGREDIENTS

3 cups (234 g) rolled oats, cooked according to directions
2 cups (450 g) cooked ground turkey
2 tbsp (30 ml) olive oil
1/2 cup (75g) chopped cooked carrots
1/2 cup (85 g) chopped cooked zucchini
A sprinkle of dried or finely chopped fresh parsley and rosemary

DIRECTIONS

1. Cook the rolled oats according to directions and set aside to cool.
2. Combine the cooked ground turkey and olive oil in a large mixing bowl.
3. Add the chopped carrots and zucchini to the bowl.
4. Mix in the cooked rolled oats.
5. Add a sprinkle of dried or finely chopped fresh parsley, rosemary, and oil to the mixture and stir well.
6. Store the dog food in an airtight container in the refrigerator for up to 3 days.

NOTES

(150 kcal per 1/2 cup)

CHICKEN AND RICE WITH CHEESE

SERVINGS: 4
PREPPING TIME: 10 MIN
COOKING TIME: 25 MIN

INGREDIENTS

1 1/3 cups (300 g) of chicken
1 cup (120 g) of rice
1 cup (200 g) of mashed sweet potato
4 tbsp (60 g) Grated Cheese
4 cups (950 ml) of water

DIRECTIONS

1. Combine chicken and water in a pot, then reduce heat and simmer for 20-25 minutes until the chicken is cooked.
2. Remove the chicken from the pot and shred it into small pieces.
3. In the same pot, add rice and simmer for 15-20 minutes until it is cooked.
4. Add the shredded chicken, mashed sweet potato, and grated cheese to the pot, and simmer for a few minutes until everything is heated through.
5. Remove from heat and drain off most of the liquid.
6. Allow to cool and stir in the liquid.
7. Store in an airtight container in the refrigerator for up to three days or freeze for longer storage.

NOTES

(250 kcal per serving)

CHICKEN AND RICE PORRIDGE

SERVINGS: 6-8
PREPPING TIME: 10 MIN
COOKING TIME: 25 MIN

INGREDIENTS

12oz (340 g) boneless, skinless chicken breasts
1 cup (185 g) white rice
4 cups (960 ml) low-sodium chicken broth
1 cup (150 g) grated carrots
1 tbsp (15 ml) olive oil

DIRECTIONS

1. Cut the chicken breasts into small pieces and set them aside.
2. In a large pot, combine the uncooked rice and chicken broth.
3. Bring the mixture to a boil, reduce the heat to low, and simmer for 10 minutes.
4. Add the chicken pieces and grated carrots to the pot.
5. Simmer for 15-20 minutes or until the chicken is cooked and the rice is tender.
6. Mash the chicken and rice into a porridge-like consistency.
7. Allow the porridge to cool before serving your dog.

NOTES

(150 kcal per serving)

TURKEY AND CARROT MASH

SERVINGS: 2
PREPPING TIME: 10 MIN
COOKING TIME: 00 MIN

INGREDIENTS

1/2 lb (225 g) cooked ground turkey
1/2 cup (75 g) mashed carrots
1/4 cup (60 ml) low-sodium chicken broth
1/2 tbsp (7.5 ml) olive oil
1/8 tsp (0.6 ml) dried parsley

DIRECTIONS

1. Combine the cooked ground turkey, mashed
   cooked carrots, low-sodium chicken broth, olive oil, and dried parsley in a mixing bowl.
2. Stir everything together until well combined and the mixture has a mash-like consistency.
3. Allow the mash to cool before serving your dog.

NOTES

(190 kcal per serving)

SALMON AND RICE PORRIDGE

SERVINGS: 2
PREPPING TIME: 10 MIN
COOKING TIME: 10 MIN

INGREDIENTS

4 oz (113 g) canned salmon
1/2 cup (100 g) cooked white rice
1/2 cup (120 ml) low-sodium chicken broth
1/2 tbsp (7 ml) olive oil

DIRECTIONS

4. Combine the canned salmon, white rice, low-sodium chicken broth, and olive oil in a small pot.
5. Cook over medium-low heat, stirring frequently, until the mixture has a porridge-like consistency.
6. Allow the porridge to cool before serving your dog.

NOTES

(180 kcal per serving)

 **CHAPTER 7**

DIET MANAGEMENT AND PICKY EATERS

TIPS FOR MANAGING YOUR DOG'S DIET

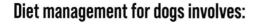

Diet management for dogs involves:

- Choosing the right food.
- Determining the appropriate portion sizes.
- Establishing a consistent feeding schedule.

To ensure a balanced diet, select high-quality ingredients containing essential nutrients for your dog's overall health.

To determine the appropriate amount of food for your dog, you can use the following formula: take your dog's weight in kilograms, multiply by 30, and add 70 (or, take their weight in pounds, divide by 2.2, multiply this figure by 30, and add 70).

This calculation will help you estimate your dog's daily caloric needs, which can be adjusted based on age, activity level, and specific dietary requirements.

Feeding schedules play a crucial role in diet management. For most pet dogs, feeding once or twice per day is recommended. Many dogs will benefit from eating equally divided meals two to three times per day. However, it's essential to consult with your veterinarian to determine the best feeding schedule and meal plan tailored to your dog's individual needs.

CONCLUSION

EMBRACING A FRESH FOOD LIFESTYLE FOR YOUR DOG

Many pet parents are starting to embrace a fresh food lifestyle for their dogs and for good reason. Dogs, like humans, thrive on a varied and nutritious diet, and feeding them fresh, whole foods can help ensure they get the nutrients they need to lead long, healthy lives.

Home-cooked meals are an excellent way to ensure nutrient diversity in your dog's diet. You can customize the ingredients with a home-cooked meal to suit your dog's nutrient needs. Additionally, home-cooked meals for dogs have many benefits, including:

Control over Ingredients: You have complete control over ingredients by preparing your dog's meals at home. You can choose high-quality, whole foods that provide nutrients without harmful additives or fillers. This way, you can avoid feeding your dog processed foods with high sodium, sugar, and other unhealthy ingredients.

Cost-Effective Home-cooked meals for dogs: This can actually be a cost-effective alternative to store-bought kibble. Although home-cooked meals require a little more effort and time, you can save money by buying ingredients in bulk and preparing meals in large batches.

Fewer Allergies and Sensitivities: Some dogs are sensitive to certain ingredients in commercial dog food, such as grains, soy, or artificial preservatives. By preparing your dog's meals at home, you can avoid these ingredients, reducing the risk of food sensitivities and allergies.

Enhanced Flavor and Palatability: Home-cooked dog meals can be more flavorful and palatable than commercial dog food. When you cook for your dog, you can incorporate natural flavorings like herbs and spices to enhance the taste and smell of food.

THE LONG-TERM BENEFITS OF A FRESH FOOD DIET

One of the main benefits of a fresh food diet for dogs is that it can help improve their overall health and well-being. Many commercial dog foods are high in processed ingredients and preservatives, which can lead to health problems like obesity, diabetes, and digestive issues.

On the other hand, fresh foods are generally free from these harmful additives and can provide a wide range of nutrients that can help keep your dog healthy and happy.

Another benefit of a fresh diet is that it can help improve your dog's coat, skin, and teeth. Fresh foods like meat, fish, eggs, and vegetables are rich in essential fatty acids, vitamins, and minerals that help keep your dog's coat shiny and healthy. These same nutrients can also help improve skin health and reduce the risk of dental problems like gum disease and tooth decay.

A fresh diet can also benefit dogs with specific health conditions. For example, dogs with allergies, food sensitivities, or digestive issues may benefit from a fresh food diet that is free from common allergens like wheat, corn, and soy.

Similarly, dogs with kidney disease or other chronic conditions may benefit from a diet tailored to their needs, including fresh, high-quality ingredients.

STORAGE

Storing freshly cooked dog food can be easy if you follow simple steps. Most homemade dog food recipes can be safely stored in the refrigerator for 3-5 days as long as they are in an airtight container.

When storing dog food, it's important to ensure the container is airtight to maintain freshness and prevent contamination. If you plan to store the food longer, consider freezing it. Freezing dog food is an excellent option, as lower temperatures prevent bacteria from flourishing. You can realistically keep dog food in the freezer for several months.

To make it more convenient, you can portion the dog food into individual bags, remove the excess air, and let it freeze. This way, you can easily thaw and serve the food to your furry friend whenever needed. Remember to label the bags with the date and contents, so you know when to use or discard them.

Storing freshly cooked dog food is a simple process. Keep it in an airtight container in the refrigerator for 3-5 days or freeze it for more extended storage. Your dog will surely appreciate the delicious and well-preserved homemade meals you provide!

THANK YOU FOR READING MY COOKBOOK

As we conclude this cookbook journey, I want to extend my deepest gratitude to you, the reader, for your support and dedication to providing your furry companions with wholesome, homemade meals. Your love for your dogs is evident in your desire to nourish them with the best possible food, ensuring their health and happiness.

Your trust in our recipes and guidance means the world to me. We hope that the dishes you've created with my cookbook have not only delighted your dogs' taste buds but also strengthened the bond between you and your beloved pets.

By sharing these recipes with your dogs, you are not only improving their well- being but also promoting a healthier lifestyle for your entire family. As you continue to cook for your canine companions, may you find joy and satisfaction in watching them thrive and flourish with each nutritious meal.

Once again, thank you for choosing my cookbook for dogs. We wish you and your furry family members many happier, tail-wagging moments around the dinner table.

With warmest regards,

Tessa Marks

NOTES

NOTES

NOTES